Bailey's Book:
A Community Celebrates Its Assets

Bailey's Book: A Community Celebrates Its Assets

Copyright © 2010 by the BeGood Foundation

ISBN: 978-0-9827965-0-4

This book was published in the United States of America
by The BeGood Foundation

Foreword

Although our daughter Bailey's time on Earth was very short, during that time, she led an incredibly rich and abundant life. Rich and abundant because along the way she met and interacted with many wonderful people who helped enrich, nurture, and shape her into the person she was by the time she graduated from high school.

Bailey had many loyal and spirited friends along the way, from pre-school up through her senior year. She had caring teachers whom she loved and admired. There were many dedicated and generous coaches and teammates who encouraged and blessed her in so many ways, from her early attempts at softball and soccer and on through to dance, ice-skating, field hockey, and cheerleading. Her church family built her up and modeled important values which assisted in giving her a meaningful and loving framework as she approached adulthood. Family, and family friends simply loved and encouraged her. To all of these people we want to say, *"Thank you!"* Bailey was a strong and confident person as a result of all these wonderful, caring relationships. Please know that *you* made a difference in her life.

Bailey's Book: A Community Celebrates its Assets is the direct result of many generous donors who demonstrated their support for our family after Bailey's tragic accident. Donations in Bailey's name went not only to the Fairport High School Scholarship program, funding several generous scholarships, but also to the Fairport Developmental Asset Initiative, a program Bailey had enjoyed and been a part of for several years. A group of interested students and citizens came together to determine how to best use those funds to support the asset program; the result is this book, which is based on community-generated content. We want to thank everyone involved with this project, starting with all of the generous donors. The Fairport Central School District embraced the project and many administrators, teachers, and students participated in the various stages of this process. A dedicated, core group of individuals met regularly to help with decisions and the tremendous work it took to bring this project to fruition.

This book is a wonderful example of a community's strength and caring and we would like to once again thank everyone for their heartfelt concern and support.

Michael, Sharon, and Spencer Goodman

Table of Contents

Empowerment

Boundaries and Expectations

Positive Identity

118

About Bailey Goodman

We all know people who make us better for having known them. For many, Bailey Goodman was one of those rare people. And while perfect relationships are hard to find, Bailey had a way of making you think that the one you two shared was one of the few perfect ones.

Bailey had enough love and compassion to make even the most nerve-wracking situations seem positive. Her outlook on life was a unique one that most people are not lucky enough to share.

Bailey adored her family, cared deeply for her friends, and made everything she encountered seem amazingly fun. She was always determined, at times sarcastic, and constantly finding excuses to shop 'til she dropped.

While she knew the world was not perfect, Bailey worked to make it a better place while in the classroom, as an athlete, and as a leader with the Fairport-Perinton Healthy Communities-Healthy Youth Developmental Assets® Initiative.

Bailey and her friends Hannah Congdon, Meredith McClure, Sara Monnat, and Katie Shirley died on June 26, 2007, in an automobile accident. All five girls, our five Fairport Angels, will never be forgotten.

About the Fairport-Perinton Healthy Communities-Healthy Youth Developmental Assets® Initiative

By Debra Tandoi, Fairport-Perinton Asset-Building Coordinator

Eleven years ago our community dedicated its path to the developmental assets for positive youth development.

Through 50 years of extensive research on the healthy development of youth, nationally-recognized Search Institute identified 40 developmental assets that are critical for a young person's successful growth and development. These assets are positive experiences, opportunities, and personal qualities that all youth need to be responsible, successful, and caring.

The Fairport Central School District, the Town of Perinton, and the Village of Fairport joined in partnership to focus on building developmental assets for all Fairport-Perinton youth though the "Healthy Communities-Healthy Youth" initiative. We wrote a resolution declaring that the best way to ensure the healthy development of our youth and to give them a successful future is to work together on this vision. All citizens were encouraged to participate. Now, our adults, youth, schools, congregations, civic organizations, businesses, government, law enforcement, and neighborhoods work together for youth. This is the reason for our success.

The caring throughout our community is incredible. The nurturing culture is alive and well. People of all ages are connecting. Reports on our Youth Risk Behavior Survey continue to show a decrease in youth high-risk behaviors. Youth are participating in more opportunities to serve others. Senior citizens are coming to schools to interact with students. Peers are teaching peers about the value of respecting each other and others' feelings.

We have come together as a community.

So, when we lose one of our youth, we all lose that child. On June 26, 2007, we lost five together – two of our asset development initiative leaders, Bailey Goodman and Hannah Congdon, and three of their dear friends: Meredith McClure, Sara Monnat, and Katie Shirley.

This book, funded by contributions in Bailey's honor, helps us recognize Bailey's contribution to our program's success. We invited our community to help us create it by submitting stories around the 40 assets you'll find on the next page. As you read the contributions of students, teachers, and community members, we hope you are encouraged to focus on helping all youth succeed through the positive approach of building assets. We also hope that sharing our stories in this book continues to keep Bailey's spirit, and the spirit of caring, alive.

The 40 Developmental Assets

All of the content in this book relates to at least one of these 40 developmental assets identified by the Search Institute. They are the basis of the Fairport-Perinton Healthy Communities-Healthy Youth Developmental Assets® Initiative.

40 Developmental Assets®

Search Institute® has identified the following building blocks of healthy development—known as Developmental Assets®—that help young people grow up healthy, caring, and responsible.

External Assets

Support
1. **Family support**—Family life provides high levels of love and support.
2. **Positive family communication**—Young person and her or his parent(s) communicate positively, and young person is willing to seek advice and counsel from parents.
3. **Other adult relationships**—Young person receives support from three or more nonparent adults.
4. **Caring neighborhood**—Young person experiences caring neighbors.
5. **Caring school climate**—School provides a caring, encouraging environment.
6. **Parent involvement in schooling**—Parent(s) are actively involved in helping young person succeed in school.

Empowerment
7. **Community values youth**—Young person perceives that adults in the community value youth.
8. **Youth as resources**—Young people are given useful roles in the community.
9. **Service to others**—Young person serves in the community one hour or more per week.
10. **Safety**—Young person feels safe at home, school, and in the neighborhood.

Boundaries & Expectations
11. **Family boundaries**—Family has clear rules and consequences and monitors the young person's whereabouts.
12. **School Boundaries**—School provides clear rules and consequences.
13. **Neighborhood boundaries**—Neighbors take responsibility for monitoring young people's behavior.
14. **Adult role models**—Parent(s) and other adults model positive, responsible behavior.
15. **Positive peer influence**—Young person's best friends model responsible behavior.
16. **High expectations**—Both parent(s) and teachers encourage the young person to do well.

Constructive Use of Time
17. **Creative activities**—Young person spends three or more hours per week in lessons or practice in music, theater, or other arts.
18. **Youth programs**—Young person spends three or more hours per week in sports, clubs, or organizations at school and/or in the community.
19. **Religious community**—Young person spends one or more hours per week in activities in a religious institution.
20. **Time at home**—Young person is out with friends "with nothing special to do" two or fewer nights per week.

Internal Assets

Commitment to Learning
21. **Achievement Motivation**—Young person is motivated to do well in school.
22. **School Engagement**—Young person is actively engaged in learning.
23. **Homework**—Young person reports doing at least one hour of homework every school day.
24. **Bonding to school**—Young person cares about her or his school.
25. **Reading for Pleasure**—Young person reads for pleasure three or more hours per week.

Positive Values
26. **Caring**—Young person places high value on helping other people.
27. **Equality and social justice**—Young person places high value on promoting equality and reducing hunger and poverty.
28. **Integrity**—Young person acts on convictions and stands up for her or his beliefs.
29. **Honesty**—Young person "tells the truth even when it is not easy."
30. **Responsibility**—Young person accepts and takes personal responsibility.
31. **Restraint**—Young person believes it is important not to be sexually active or to use alcohol or other drugs.

Social Competencies
32. **Planning and decision making**—Young person knows how to plan ahead and make choices.
33. **Interpersonal Competence**—Young person has empathy, sensitivity, and friendship skills.
34. **Cultural Competence**—Young person has knowledge of and comfort with people of different cultural/racial/ethnic backgrounds.
35. **Resistance skills**—Young person can resist negative peer pressure and dangerous situations.
36. **Peaceful conflict resolution**—Young person seeks to resolve conflict nonviolently.

Positive Identity
37. **Personal power**—Young person feels he or she has control over "things that happen to me."
38. **Self-esteem**—Young person reports having a high self-esteem.
39. **Sense of purpose**—Young person reports that "my life has a purpose."
40. **Positive view of personal future**—Young person is optimistic about her or his personal future.

Write a Letter to Someone Special

Bailey's letter to her brother Spencer reminds us of the importance of telling the important people in our lives how much they mean to us. Use this page to write a letter to someone special in your life.

Dear _____,

_____

_____

_____

_____

_____

_____

_____

_____

_____

_____

_____

_____

A Letter from Bailey to Her Favorite Brother

Dear Spencer,

First off, I wanted to let you know how much I love you! I would like to thank you for being so protective of me throughout the years. At first and especially when I was younger I recall getting really mad at you about it, I hated it. I remember one time when I had older boys over to the house, you stormed off in a tantrum and sent your best friend over to "look for his keys" when in reality, he was sent over to spy on us. That really aggravated me. Now that I think back on it I secretly loved it because you made me feel important to you and that was the first time I realized that you love me. <u>I really appreciate you looking out for me and protecting me!</u> Thank you so much for sticking up for me all the times your friends would say inappropriate things about me to you. But most of all, thanks for being my brother!

<3 your favorite sister

To My Beautiful Daughter, Bailey Catena,

Every child at some point will ask the question, "Mom and Dad, how did you decide on my name?" I have been looking forward to the day when I could share with you the story of a student of mine, Bailey Goodman.

During my second year of teaching, I looked up at a group of girls that were entering my math class. Each one was wearing a smile that reached from one end of my classroom to the other. I knew right then and there that this was going to be a great year. Bailey Goodman stood out from the rest of my students. She would bounce into my classroom everyday with the kind of energy and enthusiasm that teachers can only dream of. She was truly a joy to teach.

While Bailey was polite and friendly to me, it was obvious that math was not her favorite subject. Despite this, Bailey and I formed a relationship with each other that went beyond the classroom. We would laugh and tell stories to one another. I even told her how much I loved her name. I said, "If I have a little girl someday, I would love to name her Bailey." She laughed and said, "My cheerleading coach says the same thing to me. I guess that everyone just loves me!" She was so right.

I loved Bailey for the positive attitude that she had towards life. She searched for the best in everyone and carried such a strong value system, even though she was only 13 at the time I taught her. Your dad even got the chance to meet Bailey Goodman when we went together on the eighth grade trip to Washington, DC. Bailey ended up in his group and he could finally understand all of my stories that I had told him at the dinner table. Bailey touched his life in just the three short days that they spend together.

As I stood at Bailey's high school graduation, I couldn't have been more proud. The fact that she wanted her middle school teachers to be there was the ultimate compliment that we could receive. She had grown into such a mature, beautiful woman. Her smile was once again a true indication of her accomplishments.

The week that I found out I was pregnant, Bailey Goodman was in a fatal car accident. At the time, I had no idea if you were a boy or girl. My conversations with Bailey kept replaying in my head throughout that week. Your dad and I talked about Bailey and what a wonderful young lady she was. We decided that if you were a girl then your name would have to be "Bailey."

The day that you were born, I kept thinking and hoping that Bailey was up in heaven smiling. I was finally able to repay her the ultimate compliment. I looked into your eyes that day and wished a million things for you in life. But, most of all, I wished that you had had the opportunity to meet the wonderful young lady whose name you carry.

Love Always,
Mom and Dad
(Sarah and Gary Catena)

Bailey Goodman

By Ally Dorsey

Bailey Goodman was a senior in 2007
She now along with 4 other girls is smiling in heaven
She was killed in a car crash late at night
She loved and treasured each and every time she could write
She was interested in school and the 40 assets
She tried to follow them and never did she forget
These assets show you how to live a positive lifestyle
It pays off in the long run, definitely worthwhile

Some of these assets are
Creative activities; do theatre, art, or play the guitar
Another asset is to read for pleasure
You may find books to become a treasure
A third asset on the list is to have a high self-esteem
Your confidence in yourself should be extreme
Asset number 32 is to know your plans in advance
If you are unprepared no one will give you a chance
Number 10 on the list is an important one; to be protected
If you are unsafe things will happen that you never expected
Asset number 26 is to be caring
Have patience, helping, and always sharing
To do homework is asset number 23
Spend time working or studying, not watching TV

Bailey Goodman followed all these assets
She left this Earth with few regrets
She influenced in our communities, in more than one way
She had a smile on her face day after day
She lit up a room with her personality
She made you laugh, I think everyone could agree
She was always an upbeat, positive person
Bailey enjoyed life but also finished everything she had begun
She wanted to make a difference in her time on Earth
She was determined to help in someway from her birth
Bailey Goodman was a great student, her future very bright
But it all came an end, that tragic, tragic night

40 Assets

By Bianca Quintero

Tiempo Libre

By Matt Yang, Tanner Gosda, Derek Gonyeo, Kyle Ronald

T ener responsabilidad
I ntegridad es importante
E mpezar llevarse bien con los démas
M otivación por sus metas
P oder personal
O tras relaciones con adultos

L ímites vecinales
I gualdad y justicia social
B uscar por oportunidades en la comunidad
R escatar personas que necesitan ayuda
E star alegre siempre

Diversidad

By Lauren Lesniewski, Miranda Sambuchi, and Allison Giambattista

Comunicarse con los amigos, los maestros, y los profesores

Otros adultos en tu vida para pasar un rato

Motivación para sacar buenas notas

Universal preocupación por los demás

No tener influencias negativas

Integridad por todas situaciones

Drogas no son importantes en nuestras vidas

Alta auto-estima

Diversidad con todo el mundo

Support

"Coach has shown me that hard work pays off."

Bailey Goodman

The Good Die Young

By Meghan Shortsleeve

On February 25th, 2004, it was a cold winter morning and I had to wake up earlier than usual to catch the fifth-grade band bus. I went into my little 7-year-old brother's bedroom and said goodbye. But little did I know that it would be the last time.

Sean was a happy-go-lucky, smiley, grateful second grader. The day my life began to change was the eve of February 24th. Sean came home from school with a sharp pain on his right side. My mom decided that we would wait a little while longer then see how he was feeling. He ended up waking up at midnight and my mom and brother went to the ER. In the morning when I woke up, the two were home safely. My mom told me that the doctors took x-rays and said that he just had constipation, and that he'd be all right. So I got my baritone horn, backpack and ski club supplies and said goodbye to Sean and headed out to the early bus.

That night, I returned home at around 9 o'clock to realize my grandparents' car was in the driveway. Confused, I walked inside and found my family all in the kitchen crying. Being the curious 10-year-old that I was, I asked what was wrong. My mother replied, "Meghan, Sean is in heaven now…" I screamed and blacked out. Later that night I found out that my little brother had been diagnosed with Meningo-coccal meningitis. He died a few hours after he was diagnosed.

During the funeral service and the calling hours, I learned that there are so many people who love and support me. I had never experienced what a support circle was before this, but while it was going on, I could see one forming before my eyes. I have learned so much about how to support others and myself through this experience. I have also learned the other aspects that play a role in support: love and loyalty.

Since then my life has changed a significant amount. I have a group of friends who understand the hardships and difficulties I go through day-to-day, and a loving family that supports me with all I do. And I go through every day knowing that Sean is still with me, through spirit, the greatest kind of support anyone could ever have. Knowing that I have all this support has made living life much easier. I will always miss Sean, but knowing that I have such a strong support circle, I can accept the fact that Sean is in a better place now.

An Unexpected Love

By Sarah Burzynski

You'd expect someone who loves you,

To announce it to the world.

Anyone of human kind,

A grandma, boy or girl.

You'd expect someone who loves you,

Would let your imagination take flight.

And say "good job" or "that could work",

And tell you that all your dreams are within sight.

You'd expect someone who loves you,

Would say that you're the best.

And hold you close and hold you near,

Closer than all the rest.

And if indeed that person loves you,

They'd say it loud and say it proud.

And when you did reach success,

They'd surely begin to dance about.

All these prove that someone loves you,

For it is very hard to love without these qualities.

But there is just one exception, you see,

And the only people who will know, is now you and

Me.

For most show their love,

Through gestures and words.

One species shows their love,

Without being heard.

They kiss your cheek,

And listen the best.

They always *try* to obey their master,

Though at times may seem a pest.

Dogs are the one exception,

Pups, Doggies, whatever you call them.

They're always there wagging their tail,

And always let you shake their paw.

Their gleeful, panting smile, always for you,

Their ears open to listen, too.

About your problems, stories, or jokes,

No matter what, they're there for you.

Dogs love you there or here,

And begin to whimper when you're not near.

When the door knob turns and you return home,

They'll jump up on you, because they love you so dear.

As you can see, dogs share a silent love,

Buddy, the retriever, even Venus the mutt.

Whatever the size or breed,

The love in your heart is unlocked and freed.

The ones you'd least expect,

Share an unbreakable friendship full of love, now hear,

D.O.G.S.

Lovers of the year!

In Honor of Bailey's Dog, Murphy

A Letter to My Dad

By Alex DeMott

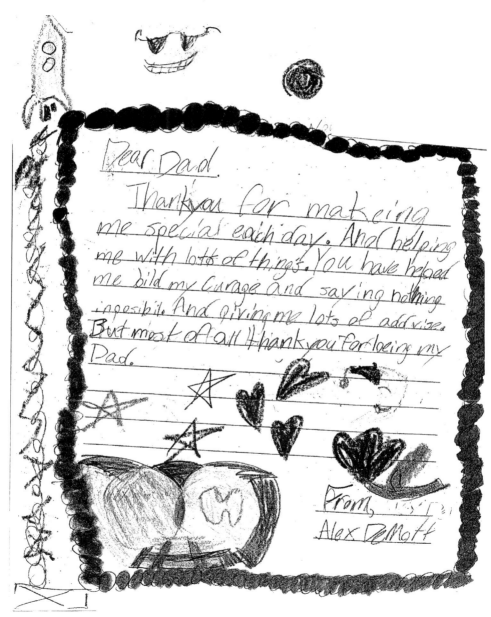

Dear Dad,

Thank you for makeing me special each day. And helping me with lots of things. You have helped me bild my curage and saying nothing inposibil. And giving me lots of addvise. But most of all thank you for being my Dad.

From,
Alex DeMott

The Last Christmas

by Renee Santoleri

(Bailey's Eighth Grade Social Studies Teacher)

(**Foreword**: When thinking about Bailey Goodman, so much comes to mind. Bailey had so many amazing qualities, but one that I remember most clearly is her love for her family and the support they gave her. Before I knew Bailey, I knew her brother, Spencer. I had taught Spencer a few years before. The first day I met Bailey, she bounced into the classroom and asked me if I remembered him. Bailey absolutely adored her brother. So often we look for heroes in the media. We look for sports stars and Hollywood icons. Often times, the real heroes are right next to us, often in our own families. For Bailey, it was Spencer, for me it was my Grandmother.)

From as early as I can remember, these were the words that my Grandma Gina would tell me every holiday season. The promise would always come late on Christmas Eve, after we had spent hours together, eating fruit and chestnuts and opening presents, Grandma would get in the car to be taken home and she would give me a kiss and say, "Goodbye Renee, this is the last Christmas that you will see Grandma."

I quickly realized as I began to age, that Grandma wasn't going anywhere and I would reply to her statement, "Yeah, yeah Grandma, I'll see you soon." When one takes a close look at my grandmother's past, you can understand why the words were always said.

My grandmother grew up in a small, poor town in Italy. Her father was an abusive man and her mother, whom she adored, would be afflicted with hearing and sight loss early on, which impaired communication between her and my grandmother across an ocean. She left Italy and came to America, after marrying her husband. She had four sons, Ralph, Mario, Mike and Jim. Shortly after losing one of her sons, Mario, at age 17, in a tragic car accident, her marriage ended in a bitter divorce. Left alone, without a strong hold on the English language, she provided the best life that she could for her and her family.

Besides all of the emotional heartache, my grandmother was also afflicted with constant physical ailments. She spent years in and out of the hospital. She managed to survive breast and lung cancers, heart bypasses, hip and knee replacements, and crippling arthritis. She often joked that she had so many surgeries in her lifetime, that she had more stitches than Frankenstein!

Yet despite all of her hurt and pain, when I think of my grand-mother, I do not think of bitterness or anger. I think of a woman who had tremendous strength and love. My grandmother loved God and her family more than anything in the world. She filled her small apartment with pictures of her children, grandchildren and great-grandchildren. For our birthdays, she would always send us all cards that would arrive at the house on the exact day. Inside, would be a crisp $5.00 bill. We would always tell her she shouldn't send us money in the mail, but it always made it to us. She would sign the cards with a paragraph of I love yous before she signed her name to it.

Grandma Gina was an amazing crocheter and knitter. She made all of us beautiful blankets, bonnets and booties. She loved watching her soap operas and eating Italian food. She would mispronounce English words, like calling string beans, screen beans. When we would correct her, she would start laughing so hard that her hearing aid would beep and then she would laugh even harder! For me, Grandma was all about joy.

When I wrote this, my grandmother was lying in hospice care, awaiting her final breaths. We had all just been together two days before, celebrating her 85th birthday. She said she didn't want to live past 80. It was too long for her, but she did! I didn't think that her passing would come as quickly as it did, but one never knows the time. In my crying and laughing, while thinking of all of the memories, I realized that the date was December 16th. I believe that after 36 years of hearing it, Grandma did get it right this time. It would be the "Last Christmas" with her, but all of the love and memories from her will be with us forever.

The Love of a Family

By Amber Bennett

My family is my support group, my team, and my closest group of friends. They help me grow, keep me stable, and brighten my day. In the picture, I am represented as the flower. I am big and strong because of my family. My mom and dad are like my stem or my roots because they support me the most out of anyone I know. Christopher, my oldest brother, is the watering can. He teaches me through both lecture and example the tools that I need to become the best person and student I can. Steven, my other older brother, brightens my day and keeps my spirits up no matter what happens. He is happy and positive at all times, and he is truly like a ray of sunshine in my life. Without my family, I would be like one of the stems that have not yet bloomed. I have been lucky to have such a terrific family because they have allowed me to become a developed and bright person.

My Hero's My Grandma

By Angela Ryck

My hero's my grandma; she smiles all day

She warms our hearts; like a summer night in May.

She always told me to just do my best

To love myself, and to love the rest.

My hero's my grandma; she's the best cook around.

Her food brings all the family into town.

She always told me to eat plenty each meal

The more pasta I eat, the better I'll feel.

My hero's my grandma; she's an old Italian lady

She passes on traditions- they'll last forever just maybe.

Her past is inspiring, though a mystery for some

Her stories will be told to generations to come.

My hero's my grandma; she's a joker for sure

"The sillier the better," is the way with her

She jokes and she giggles right out loud

She always told me no crying aloud.

My hero's my grandma; her health is not good

If I could sacrifice anything for her, I most certainly would.

But she still lives life to the fullest each day

I wish that my grandma was here to stay.

All of the Things I Didn't Say

By Megan Olivia Young

Dear Mom,

As I move through my senior year of high school, I realize just how precious time is. And I also realize how important the people in my life are and how much of an impact they have had on me. You, mom, are the biggest influence in my life and that influence has shaped me into the adult I am today. I want to thank you for all the sacrifices you've made for me. When my father left you, you had me. A tiny baby and no place of our own to go. But you worked through that and pulled yourself and me through the struggles we faced and you have become the most successful women I have ever seen. You have a great job and you love what you do. You have a house and car of your own and you have three beautiful children and a wonderful family. The love you have given me and the lessons you have taught me are the ones that stick and are the ones I always remember. You taught me that being me is the most important thing I can do. That I should never let somebody tear me down and that I am a wonderful person. You taught me honesty, respect, loving and giving, courage, and humility. You have taught me so many important lessons and have instilled in me a strong, independent, down to earth woman who knows that she can be whoever she wants to be. Thank you mom for pulling through that hard time and thank you for never giving up on me, especially in those first years where it was that much harder to take care of me because we were alone. Thank you mom, for never letting me be less than my best, and for being my biggest supporter. I love you mom.

Megan

My Dad

By Ariel L. Gladstone

By: Ariel Gladstone

My Dad

My dad is special because he helps me in a lot of ways. Here are a few. he plays with me, he helps me with my homework, and lots of other things.

I look up to my dad because he has accomplished a lot.

He also helps me with my music. He tells me if I'm off pitch and he tells he tells me if I'm just right, and so on.

He always tells me the truth.

I also think I am going to ask him for guitar lessons.

I love my dad so much!

The end. :)

I Am From

By Mark Lukenbill

I am from my home, from the room facing the backyard

and the summer sun,

from the park two streets down

and born with the urge to run through it unencumbered by more
pressing duties

I am from having the entire neighborhood in my backyard

from innocent summer games turned fiercely competitive

raised by and alongside my brother, confederate and occasional
adversary

taught by parents, neighbors, friends and innumerable relatives

I am from days of rabid, unchecked originality,

youthful verve

and creativity that is startling in retrospect

home movies that have become celluloid opuses

and invented games that no longer make sense

I am from the world as it is seen from the peaks of mountains

and reflected off the surface of lakes

free, pure, uncurbed, and unrestrained

I am from the lessons learned from youth and those who taught them

from experiences alive in memories

inspired by true events on movie screens

and the words of the great philosopher David J. Matthews

I am coming slow but speeding

I am from the past tense, looking forward...

My Family Cares About Me

By Maya Pazmiño

Maya pazmiño age 7

This is how I know my family cares about me. When they kiss me it makes me feel loved. When they hug me I feel relaxed. When they put me to bed it makes me feel good. When they let me go out side it makes me happy. Whe they let us go to the toy store it makes me feel supreised. When they buy us cothes it makes me feel speshall. When they buy me toys it makes me great. When they feed me it makes me feel well. When they read to me it makes me feel super. Thats how can tell thay love me.

My Brother

By Marni Glickman

Anyone who has an older sibling looks up to them in some way. You have a relationship with them and that sibling rivalry. I have that with my brother but it's a little different. My brother has Asperger's Syndrome.

Asperger's Syndrome is a neurobiological disorder on the autistic spectrum. It causes him to have trouble focusing and it affects his social skills. He sometimes appears to lack in empathy. A lot of his behaviors are not under his control. He is capable of functioning in everyday life, but tends to be somewhat socially immature and may be seen by others as odd or eccentric.

He had doubts put upon him at a young age. He was put in a special education class in second grade and my parents were told he wouldn't be "college material". He struggled throughout school. When frustrated he would often have "meltdowns". He very much relied on routine and didn't do well with change. Something as simple as a fire drill would throw off his day. He would be bothered by the loud alarms which to most people this wouldn't be a big deal but it would ruin his day.

Because of his differences, he was bullied a lot. People wouldn't always understand him. He was sensitive when teased and wouldn't always handle it well. He would take certain things the wrong way. Kids would "egg" him on just because they knew it would bother him and the worst thing was that this would always get him into more trouble. I can remember being in about second or third grade and he was sitting in the back of the bus and I was in front. During the bus ride some kid was teasing him and my brother proceeded to punch him. I didn't know this was happening until he was being dragged off the bus. As I watched him being walked back into the school, the whole back of the bus was cracking up. I just didn't understand why? I always hated getting the whole "that's your brother? Wow!" kind of thing. It wasn't only his peers that would bully or tease him, but parents that wouldn't want their kids to be in his class because he is a "bad influence" on their kids, or teachers that would make situations worse. With all of the doubts and struggles that he had towards him, he proved a lot of people wrong. He has gone through a lot and has grown in to a very intelligent young man. He graduated from Fairport High School this past year and now attends St. John Fisher College on partial scholarship. He intends to major in communications and Journalism.

As with siblings in all families, I can become frustrated with my brother. I just get the feeling I need to lash out at him. Sometimes I wonder "Why is he like this?" or "Why did it have to happen to me? Why can't he be like everyone else?" but what I never realize at those moment when I am being hurtful, is that I am just like those kids in the back of the bus, I am being a bully. I can honestly say this is the number one thing in my life that I am least proud of. I myself can be bully to my own brother.

Asperger's is the part of what makes him who he is. Sure what makes him be "that weird kid", but that isn't a bad thing. I love my brother to death and even though things get frustrating at times, I wouldn't want it to be any different. It adds a spark to my life and makes everyday interesting and unpredictable. He is one of the smartest people I know. He knows everything there is to know about history, baseball and useless information. He is an amazing writer and always seems to be able to captivate people with his witty sense of humor.

My brother is an individual, he is not an illness or a condition, he isn't contagious, he doesn't need a cure, he just needs people to understand him. He is my role model and I look up to him.

Dear Mom

By Maxwell Green

663 Holsky Ln
Fairport, NY 14450
November 25, 20(

Dear Mom,
I'm sending this leter
because you make me
feel soooo soooo special
inside. When I feel bad.

love ♥
Max Green

"Since our first conversation about bringing the concept of asset building to Fairport, many of us have worked tirelessly to engage the entire community in this important effort. As a result, assets have become part of the fabric of the Fairport community. From the village, town, churches, businesses, and police, all are aware and participate in the encouragement of positive assets in our youth. As leaders, we should be doing everything in our power to make certain all youth receive the benefits of assets."

Bill Cala, Superintendent FCSD—1999-2006

"The Fairport Police Department supports asset building by working with the community to keep Fairport a safe place to live, work, visit, and raise a family. I have had the opportunity to interact with youth of our community in a myriad of situations. I have personally witnessed the impact of asset building. When people join together for a common cause there is nothing that cannot be accomplished."

Maureen Chisholm, Fairport Police Chief

Empowerment

"I wanted to be the older kid giving advice to the younger kids. I wanted to make them laugh and make them feel comfortable. I wanted to teach them valuable lessons as they did for me."

Bailey Goodman

If Only For a Moment

By Emily M. Scribner

In the spring of my junior year I, along with one of my best friends, decided to go on our school's humanitarian trip to Thailand. We knew right away that it would be an amazing experience, but I had no idea how life changing the opportunity truly would be.

I had been having a pretty overwhelming year and couldn't wait for the trip. I had found out that I would be having back surgery that next summer because of my scoliosis and was really stressed out about it. I decided that I couldn't let it hold me back on anything that I wanted to do. I wanted to experience new and exciting things. I have always believed that one should be open and try new things, never hold back because I would never know what I would be missing out on. Most importantly one of my most important values in life is having the ability to help others and as soon as I heard about the orphanages we would be visiting, I knew this was exactly what I wanted to do.

Our group took a 17-hour flight to Bangkok and was able to stay with a family and learn all about the Thai culture. Over the rest of the week we would visit multiple orphanages. I was sort of nervous at first because I knew the kids wouldn't know any English. As soon as we met the kids though it didn't matter at all; all of my nerves went away instantly. At each orphanage the kids, ranging in ages from a few months to 18 years, would run over and grab my hand. I felt so welcomed just seeing the huge smiles that our group was able to put on these kids' faces. The language barrier didn't even seem to exist; we could connect and have fun without even talking. It was astonishing to me that these kids had nothing. Some of them didn't even have shoes and it seemed like they could care less. These kids were just so thrilled to see us.

The day that I returned home all of my friends and family asked me about my experiences. I was absolutely speechless and felt as though I had so much to tell them. In a few of the days following the trip I happened to ironically come across this quote that really put things into perspective for me.

"In helping others, we shall help ourselves for whatever good we give out completes the circle and comes back to us." Flora Edwards

It hadn't hit me until I got home how much I take for granted every day. The things that I found stressful before, I realized that I should be more thankful for. I am so unbelievably lucky to have medical assistance available for me. Even more importantly, I have a family that loves me unconditionally. I don't have to worry about having food or cold, clean, and fresh water. These things had always just been there for me.

Having gone to Thailand, I am so grateful that I have the opportunity to share this experience with some of my classmates. I understand now that helping others is what we are meant to do. I knew that I had helped give these kids at least one good day. With all that the orphans had gone through, I was able to put a smile on their faces if only for a moment. As an individual I went on this trip to do something new. I had no idea that I would come back with memories to last me a lifetime, a whole new group of friends and a completely new perspective on how I live my life every day.

"Children fill our lives with sunshine and our hearts with love."

By Susan Reindel

For several years this quote has hung on my classroom door. It is there to remind me of the joy I feel as I enter a classroom filled with children each day. But, it is also there for the children to be reminded that I care for them. Their enthusiasm is catching. Our lives are enriched because of them. I hope your heart smiles as mine does as we appreciate the small special moments the children share with us. Children are GREAT!

Often as adults, we can become bogged down in "everyday details." Our suitcases are filled with past experiences. Children don't have a full suitcase yet. The joy they bring to us each day is a delight. Being a child can be a carefree time of life. They bounce, yell, wiggle, run, laugh and play. Children are eager to try new things. They are creative and social. Children make me excited to view the future.

Rejoice, we have children in our lives!

Let's continue to support, encourage and nurture the children in our lives.

"Children fill our lives with sunshine

and our hearts with love."

Outside My Comfort Zone

By Amanda Nozik

I was wandering around the city of Toronto with bagged lunches in my hands on a Mission trip. Each day we were given an assignment that would take us out of our comfort zone. We were to hand out these lunches to homeless people on the streets of Toronto and hopefully strike up a conversation with them. My group, consisting of four youth, came across two middle aged men who were lying on two benches covered with cardboard. They stopped us as we walked by asking if they could have some of the food we were carrying. We stopped and gave each of them a bag.

At first I was a bit hesitant to get too close and nervous to have a conversation with them. After I started talking with to them I became more and more comfortable. They were extremely nice guys, and just because they were homeless didn't give me a reason to judge them. I started talking to one of them about baseball and he thought it was awesome that I was from New York because he was a huge fan of the Yankees. His face seemed to light up more as I was talking with him and it made me realize how I was impacting this man who I didn't even know. Just the fact that I took an hour out of my day to spend time here with him meant everything to him.

I noticed a shopping cart sitting next to him full of bottles, ragged clothes, and some other random items. He reached into it and grabbed a New York Yankees baseball cap and handed it to me. He wanted to give me something for being so kind to him, but I couldn't accept it. After spending five minutes trying to convince him to keep it for himself, he finally gave in. At this moment I was overwhelmed with feelings of guilt. This man who had a fraction of what I have was willing to give away what was probably his most valuable possession. In a very short time a perfect stranger became someone he trusted and wanted to share his belongings with. This man who I would have normally run away from on the street impacted me in a way I can't explain. As we were talking some more, I saw my youth pastor signal me that I had to leave. I was sad to say goodbye to my new friend. After thanking me a million times as I was leaving, he stopped me and said, "Because I know that people like you are out there tonight, I'm going to sleep much better. May God bless you."

The Man with the Greens

By Kelsey Talty

Nervous and excited at the same time,

Stepping out of my comfort zone

And into the unfamiliar.

Images fly through my head

Of what I thought it would be like,

How I thought it would look.

Slippery, sweaty hands

Twist the door knob open, and while stepping inside,

My imaginations became a reality in that single moment.

Swiftly walking past the blur of people,

Finding my way to the back

I was greeted enthusiastically by other volunteers

A job was given to me,

I put on the gloves

And got to work.

The soup kitchen was set up like a little restaurant

Tables and chairs placed around the room

With a kitchen in the back.

Bringing the food from the kitchen to the hungry people

Was my job,

And I couldn't wait to begin.

Hot dogs, soup collard greens, water and milk

Those were the items of choice

My eager, twelve year old self, was just waiting to serve

Finally, lunch hour was beginning

From the room next to us,

What seemed like a million people, burst through the doors, ready to eat.

As I expected,

The people came to eat

Did not seem like the people who went to my school

Raggedy clothed, and dirty

Extreme skinniness

Some even disabled

Feeling bad and guilty

Yet still nonjudgmental

I began serving food

My grandpa had come with me

Serving collard greens

Was his job.

A giant bucket of water and seaweed

Or collard greens some might call

Looked like a big bowl of yuck to me

There was one man that particularly

Stood out to me

And for a small reason

Gray-haired, tall, and skinny

He was dressed in old jeans, and a faded t-shirt

Was not clearly shaven either

He had a glow in his eyes though

Always smiling

Polite to everyone in the room

Of all the food served

The seaweed looking collard greens

Was all he wanted.

I noticed him get at least six servings of the stuff

Not once did he try a hot dog

Or get a glass of water

He seemed so hungry

He definitely got his fair share of food

And he ate every bite

I watched him as he left the room

The soup kitchen was also a place where homeless people could stay

An old couch seemed to be waiting for him

Plopping himself down

He fell right to sleep

Must have been his every day routine

I felt good about myself

Helping those who couldn't afford food,

Or a place to stay

And while I had this good feeling,

I thought that the people receiving our help

Were getting more benefits from it than we were

Helping others has always been a passion of mine

And while a part of the reason I love it so much is the good feeling you get

I'm much happier knowing that the people really need that service

I'm happy knowing that someone can benefit from my time

Even as a twelve year old

I was helping the community

It's been five years since my first day at the soup kitchen

And not once,

Have I ever forgotten, the man with the greens.

Miserable

By Lauren T. Reed

That girl on the bench,

all sad and miserable.

I talk and cheer her up.

she tells her life stories,

they aren't pleasant.

hold your head up high.

believe in yourself,

like I do with myself.

so I took her hand,

gave her hope,

she smiled bright,

and joyfully skipped.

The Fairport Angels Memorial Scholarship Winner 2009

Students applying for the Five Fairport Angels Memorial Scholarship were asked to write a letter to an out-of-town friend describing the impact the tragic accident in 2007 had on the Fairport community and on them personally. They were instructed to address how the "lessons learned" from this event might have affected their relationships with others, their values, and their lives. This is the winning essay from 2009.

By Kerisa Bonville

Dear Beverly,

As you know I will be graduating this June. When I think back on my years at Fairport High School I remember five young women that had a tremendous impact on my high school, my community, and me.

It all started when I was a sophomore and I was selected to be a Leadership Asset Trainer for my school district. Through this program a team of sophomores, juniors, and seniors work together and facilitate a day of activities with freshmen to promote healthy lifestyles and encourage leadership. Each of us had our own special qualities and images that set us apart from each other. Dylan was the varsity football player, Katie was like the mom, Marcus was the musician, Heather loved pageants, Maureen was the actress, Livy sang, Alexander was the genius, and then there was Hannah and Bailey, our varsity cheerleaders.

I was one of the babies on the team because I was a sophomore and it was my first year. The seniors and juniors had established themselves within the group so being new was overwhelming. Hannah and Bailey changed that for me though. After my first facilitating experience they said they really liked me and that I was a good facilitator. They helped me feel welcomed and I started to feel like I really belonged. They were the ones who inspired me to apply for the position in the first place so I valued their compliments and admired them. Meeting with these students once a month became something that I looked forward to and made my school year fly by and soon summer had arrived.

On June 27, 2007 I started my morning routine. I poured a bowl of shredded wheat for myself and sat on the couch. I turned on the television and then set my cereal down on the end table. There was a news break that came on just as my television went from black to color. My eyes welled with water. I felt heaviness in my face and in my throat. I choked back my tears as my local news station told me that five teens from my high school had been killed in a car accident. They had not given any names yet.

As I pushed down each number on the phone pad to call my best friend I prayed that I did not know the victims. My best friend answered the phone as if she knew it was me and then I asked if she had heard. I said her to "Just please tell me the names." Very gently, she eased the names over the phone line. The night before, on June 26, 2007 Hannah and Bailey had passed away along with three of their best friends, Sara, Meredith, and Katie, in a terrible car accident.

My entire community was bleeding with remorse. Everywhere you went that day you saw the tear stricken faces. That night, I sat among thousands of people on the hill next to our school for a candle light vigil to remember our five "Angels". Our hearts were breaking in silence. Since then, that hill has been officially named "Angel Hill", and rightly so. These girls impacted thousands of people. They broke down walls between cliques in our school. There seemed to be less judgment and more support between the students.

After the accident, our 1800 student population was united more then ever before. When the girls passed away they left behind their dreams and values that have helped our community grow. The loss of our Five Fairport Angels, Katie, Meredith, Hannah, Bailey, and Sara has taught us to always be aware of the potential impact that we have on the people around us and that sometimes the smallest gesture or acknowledgement toward someone else could have an impact on their day or maybe even their life.

Personally, I have come to value the small things in life like driving to school with my best friend every morning, singing songs with my little cousins, and shopping with my mom. Most importantly, I believe the girls left behind a legacy of true leadership. Reflecting on the lives they led, the angels taught me that to be a good leader you must know how to bring leadership out in others through empowerment and support. They also taught me that a leader is someone with integrity, courage, values, selflessness, and brings about unity within a group of people, whether it is a group of ten or thousands. These aspects of their leadership helped me to grow as leader even after they passed away.

On June 26, 2008, I was asked to give a speech to the entire Fairport School District faculty as an acknowledgement to a great school year of leadership in the community. Speaking in front of a thousand people about what leadership meant to the community on the anniversary of the death of the girls who helped me find leadership within myself seemed impossible. I prayed to the girls to help me get through it. When I walked in front of the audience I felt a sudden feeling of relief and comfort. A warmth surrounded me. The audience laughed at my jokes and commended my speech. I was honored to give that speech. It was my way of honoring the girls and more importantly thanking them for helping me find my place in Leadership Asset Training.

That evening after my speech, I went to "Angel Hill" and just sat. This was my closure. I thought about how being asked to give that speech was the girls telling me I had truly become a leader in the community and that they believed in my ability to make a difference in the world and bring happiness to others. The girls have given me faith that my dream to make a positive impact on other people's lives is a reality and I will forever be grateful to them.

Love,

Kerisa

Peace

By Justin Xaisanasy

"The asset-building initiative in Fairport-Perinton has provided this area's youth with the tools and understanding to become tomorrow's leaders. By bringing together a variety of public and private leaders for the sole purpose of helping support our youth, this initiative has demonstrated how dedicated individuals, working together, can have a dramatic impact. I am proud to live in a town that has made such a strong commitment to its youth."

Assemblyman David Koon,
135th Assembly District

Boundaries and Expectations

"I have grown from a spoiled girl to someone who understands limits and sacrifices."

Bailey Goodman

Travis: a Hero to Many

By Jacqui Breese

Travis is a friend to all but a hero to many more. I've known him as long as I can remember, because our parents have been friends for many years too. Back then I didn't know he was going to be such a huge hero to everyone. He has two brothers and at one time they were all amazing football players. Although, when it comes to bravery, Travis sticks out. He fought in the Marines but he is more than just a hero, he is my friend.

I don't remember when I last saw Travis but I know it was when he was on a break from the war. Before you're able to fight though you need to go through the right training. When Travis was getting trained I wrote him a card telling him to never give up. I also wrote to not let his Generals get him down. He didn't and after training Travis learned how to do all kinds of interesting things. He learned how to use a parachute and to shoot accurately. When he learned how to jump out of an airplane he sent us a picture. It was so cool, and he was sitting on the edge almost ready to jump.

Just this year Travis and his fiancé, Leena, were planning their wedding. When they finally picked a day he received a phone call. Unfortunately, he had to go to Afghanistan. He wouldn't make it back in time for his wedding. They were devastated, but he knew what he had to do. He always puts his country first, even if he doesn't want to.

I am really proud of Travis for taking a chance. He loves his country and always will. He is no longer in the Marines and now wants to be in the Secret Service. He would like to protect our President from danger. I hope Travis knows he always helps his country. He started off just bringing me to swimming lessons, then defended his country as a Marine, and hopefully he will be in the Secret Service. He is a perfect hero to anyone who meets him.

Me and Bailey Goodman

By Julia Pieri

Bailey was a very nice girl. She always knew what to say and how to say it well. It seemed like she was always there for me. Bailey was a great role model in Fairport, NY.

When I was younger Riley baby sat me and my brother and sister. Bailey came when Riley was not available. Bailey would also show up when Riley was baby sitting so we could all spend time together.

I looked up to Bailey because she was so sweet and kind. I also knew Bailey was a cheerleader. I have become a cheerleader too. I intend to cheer for a while because I enjoy the skills I have developed. When I cheer I often think of Bailey. Bailey was an amazing writer as well. I read some of her work. I hope I can write as well as Bailey some day too.

I love Bailey Goodman so much. She was the most compassionate person I've ever met. I miss her so much. Bailey will always be in our hearts. But one of the saddest things that had to happen is that we lost Bailey and the four other Fairport angels on my birthday. I will remember them forever.

My Grandpa, My Hero

By Riley Hopkins

My hero iz my grandfather. he helpz me when I am zaad. He iz play ful. He makez me laf and he play with me zometimez he collz me tiger becaz I m wiald and carazy and he doz not carr. My favorit time iz wheen we whent to the zoo! I got a Webkinz. A webkinz iz a ztuft animal and it can go on line. It iz zo cool. And I got a oval penny. We wheen to the znake cage. We alzo wheen to the lioan. The lioan wher growling at uz but it waz fun and I got a loley pop. The loley pop waz zweet and coler. ful and varry tazty and hard and crunchy. after that we wheent to the tigerz cage! the tigerz wher growling at me caze they want my dog cuz they hate dogz. The znakz were hizing at me but it waz fun and we zaw a blue jay and a yelloy won to. it waz buutifule. I waz varry worme. So I got koool lade to cool me down it waz hot SO we got zom coold water and that coold uz down. after that we whent home.

My Role Model

By Matthew Hawk

Aunt Kate and I are pretty much best friends. Every time I could visit her I would. That's what made it so hard. It was six years ago and the phone rang. My Aunt had colon cancer.

Mom hung up the phone, sobbing. I asked her what was wrong, but all she did was frantically pace around the kitchen crying. She told me I was going over to a friend's house and she was going to my Aunt's house. In my mind I was thinking something horrific must have happened. When my Mom came home she quietly told me the news. I was going through my mind searching for the word cancer, but nothing came up. I didn't understand what was going on. Mom suddenly blurted out crying, and I joined her so I wouldn't feel left out.

Quietly, I crept into my Aunt's room at the hospital. When I looked at her she was asleep. She had a tube on her arm that looked painful. I crept over to her and sat next to her until we left. The next time my family and I visited her she was awake and peppy.

Aunt Kate had most of her colon removed, and had chemotherapy and radiation to get rid of the cancer. Right now she does not have cancer. Aunt Kate is a tennis and squash coach and because of her treatment, she cannot have children, so the children she coaches and teaches are like her own. Aunt Kate is a HUGE inspiration to me. The reason is because she was given a difficult challenge and survived! My Aunt continues to give to others, and she is my friend and role model, and I love her.

Watch Dog

By Tessa Fiscella

Big dog sits at the head of the long table

Listening to my request

Silver keys glisten in the afternoon sunlight

I watch as they drop slowly into my hands

The black truck sits idle in the drive way

"Be home by eleven" the big dog growls

The words drift after me as I bound out the front door

Freedom is mine as I rush down the winding asphalt roads

Friends greet me by the crackling bon fire

The summer sun set breaks into a starry sky

Laughter rings into the night

Time slips away with the fun we are having

I come home late

I jumped that jagged fence surrounding the big dog

My risk landed me in chains on the other side

Apology not accepted

The silver keys are taken

As the black truck sits idle in the drive

My Role Model

By Rachel White

I have many role models, but when I think of the words "role model", I think of my Aunt Margaret. She is not just a role model, but also a friend. On May 16th, 2004, my brother and I were in the midst of celebrating our first Holy Communion at our house. My cousins and I were playing in my basement, and then we were told not to come upstairs. We were all frightened and confused. What we didn't know was that pregnant aunt had gone into cardiac arrest on our kitchen floor and was being rushed to emergency.

In the cardiac department at Strong Memorial Hospital, my aunt delivered my baby cousin Jack, twelve weeks premature. She was the first person to deliver a baby in the cardiac department of the hospital. Different members of my family kept watch over her and Jack. I hadn't really understood what had happened until I went to visit her, and she didn't even remember my name or who her own children were. She suffered from heart and brain trauma. Among other problems, my cousin couldn't breathe on his own and was in the intensive care unit.

My Aunt Margaret has gone through many things in life with faith and hope. She is an inspiration and a fine example of never giving up. Sometimes when things in my lie are difficult, I think of my aunt and what she has, and still is going through. Jack passed away on January 31st, 2006 when he was two. My aunt believed that Jack helped her in her recovery, and when she was able to function properly it was time for him to go. She still struggles daily with her memory, but my whole family and I wall always love her very much. I realize now that with a little faith and positive thinking, I can get through almost anything.

My Mom, My Hero

By Holly Ness

My mom is like a guardian angel to me. She makes my fears disappear when she talks to me; my mom is my hero. She is always there for me to help me when I struggle. I look up to her as a role model and a friend.

One autumn day I sat at the kitchen table, concentrating on my script. As a lead in the school play, I was in every scene. There was no way I could memorize it all, the play was coming quickly, and I still had to remember half the script. Before I knew it, tears filled my eyes. Embarrassed and defeated I ran upstairs to my room, slammed the door, and stuffed my face in my pillow. Footsteps tapped up the stairs and somebody lightly knocked. It was Mom, she asked me if she could come in. I said no, but she came in anyway, holding my script. Mom patted me on the head until I looked up. She explained to me that I can't give up and I just have to do my best.

All of a sudden, I said my first line, and she said the next. We were up in my room practicing for at least a few hours, until I could say all of my lines, well with emotion. The big night finally came, and I didn't falter, not once! After the show, Mom gave me a big bouquet of roses and said it was the best show she's ever seen.

As I look back on that day, I realize that if Mom hadn't told me to persevere, I would have given up on a lot of other activities. Mom committed her time to help me, and I thank her for that. Some people don't understand that it's the little things in life that can make big differences. I know one thing for sure; I love my mom as wide and as endless as space and I will till the end of time.

Brother in the Navy

By Kevin Clough

by Kevin Clough

Brother in the Navy

Can you believe I have brother in the Navy? In August 2007 my brother Jon joined the United States of America Navy. Before he was really in the Navy he had to go to boot camp. Boot camp is like training for Navy people. The boot camp was in Chicago, Illinois. It was eight weeks long! After he went to boot camp he went to school to be an electrician. An electrician is a guy who works on lights and stuff like that. Today Hes stationed (The place hes staying at) in Norfolk, Virginia. I miss him so much. I went to Virgina once. I got to see his apartment and meet his roommates. I went there because.. There was an awesome commissioning ceremony for the new huge aircraft carrier that my brother gets to sleep and work on it!

My brother showed me that hes a great rolemodel. I don't want to grow up and join the Navy, but I want to go in the right direction like he did. When he was a teenager he wasn't a good kid. But now he tried to do something with his life Now just look at him! Hes wise, smart, tough, rolemodel, and he's my brother.

The End

Expectations

By Susan Reindel

I am sure many of you are familiar with the book *Where the Wild Things Are* by Maurice Sendak. In this book, the character Max visits a place where there are wild things. The wild things are being very wild, and Max has had enough.

"Now stop!" commands Max. Then he sent the wild things to bed without their supper.

Max's order to stop is powerful. Even though Max was a little boy, the wild things listened to him and followed his rule. Max shows us that it is important to have boundaries and expectations. He enforced his boundary and his expectation with the beasts. When Max said STOP, they stopped.

We need to remember the same. When someone tells us to stop bothering them, we need to stop. And when we want someone to stop bothering us, we should be able to say STOP and have the person stop bothering us. It is empowering for a child to say "STOP" when one classmate is bothering another. When Dan had a friend chasing him on the playground, and he said "STOP chasing me." The friend stopped. The boys were able to enjoy their play ground time.

Our asset of boundaries and expectations work like this.

We all have boundaries, or limits. Sometimes the boundaries are rules. Other people have expectations for us to follow the rules. We also have expectations for ourselves. We all expect to have a good day. This means, we must respect the rules or expectations we have for ourselves and others have for us.

Inspired by Jolene L. Roehlkepartain

"A community is the sum of its parts. When each part has been influenced by the building blocks of developmental assets, this creates a healthier, more caring and supportive community base."

Jim Smith,
Perinton Town Supervisor

Constructive Use of Time

"Learn it one step at a time and do it because you love it, not because it's work."

Bailey Goodman

Helping my Community

By Molly Elizabeth Coller

MOLLY coller
MR. Roʒc.... Dudley School 6/6

Hi, my name is Molly and I help my
community by: helping my
good neighbor Jill. I like buying
her food. I also keep her company.
Were BEST friends. And I mean
who says a 7 year old cant
be friends with a 90 year old
Huh? Well next time your
looking for a friend. you should
look at people that are older.

Unplugged

By Marcus J. Merriman

(This is a college entrance essay I wrote when applying to schools. I think the question must have had to do with how I gain the respect of my peers. It reminds me of Bailey because I remember her confidence and the spirit that people appreciated in her. I think that she was a great role model for me, and anyone who had the pleasure to know her.)

Guitar playing takes up most of my free time. The tips of my fingers are worn and calloused over. My thumbs are strong, and my coordination is sure, and quick. After school I sit alone in my room imitating and writing music for hours. The cushion of the black leather office chair I sit in is wrinkled, and caves into the middle. I close my eyes and calmly listen to the rhythm and melody, and I feel the emotion of the song. I imitate the song and then improvise my own guitar part. During summer I would have friends over, and under the midnight blue I would play for them. Now I enjoy playing in front of people, although it took me a while to gain that confidence.

My sophomore year, my first at the high school, I saw the performances at "Unplugged." Unplugged is similar to a talent show. During free periods student artists perform their music or poetry for other students. It's a coffee house setting. The lights are dim and shaded blue. The seats are similar to a small lecture room. Desks fold out on the sides, and the seats are in 5 rows. The rows arch around the performance floor. I remember as a sophomore admiring the performers. I respected the confidence that set the better acts apart I remember feeling relaxed if the performer was relaxed and anxious if they were nervous.

When I was a junior, a year ago, I had a couple of friends over around the campfire. It was fall, and school had been in session for about three weeks. The breeze was cool, but the fire was warm. My mom brought my guitar out, which at the time embarrassed me. I tried to refuse to play, but everyone convinced me to play just one song. I played a classical guitar song I learned while taking lessons at Eastman School of Music. I played smooth and swift, gaining confidence with each note. They begged me to play more, and I continued with more classical songs, avoiding singing. The guitar became more and more comfortable in my palms, and I eventually ran out of classical songs that I had memorized. I played some riffs of songs we all knew and from bands we all liked. Eventually I closed my eyes; I took in a slow deep breath through my nostrils and began to sing. I didn't open my eyes until I finished. When I finished, I opened my eyes and everyone gave me compliments in disbelief, never knowing I could sing too. One friend told me I had to play at the Unplugged for that year. I agreed, thinking he would forget, not really planning on following through and playing.

Spring rolled around and the sign up sheets for Unplugged were posted. I went to look at the names I recognized on the list, I looked at the names, and in two of the slots I saw my name written. I thought about crossing my name off of the list, but decided to sleep on the idea of playing. That night I lay in bed listening to the songs I could play, imagining myself at Unplugged performing them. I convinced myself to follow through with the idea and play during my study hall and lunch periods.

The days went by slower, but weeks went by faster as Unplugged approached. The butterflies, always there, and growing each day. The day finally came, then the hour, then the minute. I walked to the center, my face lit by the dim light above me. Taking deep breaths I calmed myself down. I looked at the audience, the faces I knew and the faces I didn't. Taking one last deep breath I played. The chord was awfully ugly. I realized I hadn't checked the tuning of the guitar before I played. I re-tuned the guitar frantically, and began again. I went through the progression one time before beginning to sing. Each note was more proud than the last. When I sang, each line had more emotion than the line before, gaining confidence as I continued. The song ended and the audience clapped. I smiled and thanked them, and walked off the center floor. Relieved, I put my guitar away.

Since then I have played comfortably in front of even larger audiences. I learned that it is important to take chances, but also important to work to improve my opportunity for success in those chances I take. I have grown confident and proud of whom I am, and content with the lifestyle I lead.

Continuance

By Henna Csont

Traced
In endless circles
Ceaselessly
The tick tock of the clock
Each instant
It withers away
The nebulous element of everyday life

Time

A precious gift we are granted
From God above

Time to lend a hand

Tick Tock
Time to be influential

Tick Tock

Time to revolutionize

Tick Tock

Time to ameliorate

Tick Tock

To waste the contribution
You can bestow upon society
Is absurd

Time forever passes
Use yours wisely

Cross Country

By Jenny Bruno

I ran around the final stretch of the course. The freezing rain was pushing me in the other direction. The 40 degree air had frozen me about 10 minutes ago. I persevered through the pouring rain as the finish line came into view. My legs started to move faster finding a strength I didn't think I had. Finally, I stumbled across the finish line; numb, wet and exhausted. My Mom came up to congratulate me, but my only thought was changing out of my tank top and shorts. The whole Cross Country team spent the bus ride back to Martha Brown defrosting. Through out that race I wondered to myself why I was doing this, but the sense of accomplishment I felt crossing the finish line answered my question.

Devoting my after school time and my Saturday mornings to running for a team was probably one of the best decisions I ever made. I think being on the Cross Country team has made me a much better person. I learned teamwork skills in practice and I learned perseverance and commitment in the meets. I've also met new people and became better friends with others. I will admit that I got a bit mad when I would come home to see my brother sitting and playing the computer, with all his homework done. It seemed he was being rewarded for not doing anything after school, but I had a better reward – memories. I will remember the many jokes and fun times. One thing I know I will remember is at our scrimmage my friend came in 19th place on the 19th and it was her birthday! At the McQuaid Invitational, I saw buses from as far away as Memphis and thought how cool it is to be apart of something this big. When the season ended, I realized I couldn't wait for Cross Country to begin again next year.

Summer Nights

By Erin M. Schaaf

A smile as bright as the sun
Reflects from across the fire
A laugh escapes our lips
As dusk wears into night
Nothing can bother us
Not on those beautiful, wonderful
Summer nights that last forever

Filled with smiles and laughter
With smoky logs and blazing embers
Pain holds no place in those
Summer nights that last forever

These nights set us free
From the ties of reality
From our lives we cannot stand
And let us breathe once more
Let us find me again, during those
Summer nights that last forever

The girl I love being
Comes out to play
When the shadows grow long
And friends are all I know
She hides when the sun appears
She's free during those
Summer nights that last forever

Filled with velvet skies, and crackling fires
With laughter, smiles and us
I am me and I am free
When summer nights last forever

Treasured Memories

By Kathleen Andrews

My extended family is not one that is inseparable, has weekly dinners or family game nights, or even sees each other that often. After all, my cousins and grandparents live about 5 hours away from me in opposite directions. Despite the distance we are able to come together every year on Christmas to spend some very needed time together. We only have one family tradition that has been continued since my grandparents first got married over 60 years ago.

Every year around Thanksgiving, my grandparents come to my house to make Stollen, a German Christmas bread. Making stollen is no easy task and usually takes an entire day to make, mostly due to the amount of time it takes for the bread to rise. I can remember helping my mom and my grandma make it ever since I was little, probably around 4 years old. Even now I help make sure each stollen is 11 ounces, help fold the dough into the correct shape, cover them in about 7 layers of butter and sugar, and wrap them in aluminum foil. The process is long and demanding, so much so that my dad has made his job video taping the event since that is the easier job of the two. Once each individual stollen is wrapped, about 18 or 19 loaves in all, we put half in my grandpa's attic and half in my refrigerator and they stay there until Christmas Eve.

It is traditional in Germany to not eat stollen until after midnight so that is what we do at my grandparent's house on Christmas Eve. Now as my grandparents have gotten older it has been difficult for them to stay up that late. To accommodate them, a few years ago we "switched" to Dresden time, which is about 6 hours ahead of Eastern Standard Time. This annual eating of the stollen is what Christmas with my family is all about. However, this year is different. This time around, it is no longer safe for my grandparents to travel and my family was not able to go see them at Thanksgiving. Now of course my cousins will bring stollen of their own but it is not the same at all. The 60 plus year tradition is broken. Looking back on all those late nights both before and after the bread has been completed, I think of all the memories my grandparents have given me. I'm not sure how much longer I will be able to get to see them so I am learning to treasure every moment and maybe one day I will be able to continue the tradition of stollen with my own family.

Applicants to the Bailey Goodman Memorial Scholarship Winner administered through the Dollars for Scholars Program were asked to respond to this question: *"While Bailey loved her time at Fairport High School, she was also looking forward to starting college and leaving behind many of the stereotypes, preconceived notions, and activities that defined her. As you enter college, what will you be glad to leave behind and who do you look forward to becoming?"*

This is the response written by the student who received the scholarship in 2009.

Bailey Goodman Memorial Scholarship Winner 2009 Application Essay

By Stephen Tortorella

For me, college will be a fresh start. Like Bailey, I cannot wait to get out of our sheltered, preconceived lifestyle of Fairport. I have spent my four years at FHS doing the best I can to make everyone around me feel accepted and welcome, but I still know that people pre-judge me, stereotype each other, and define their peers by views that others tell them to hold. Next year I look to begin my life, and meet the people that will allow me to further my aspirations, rather than hold me back.

Having never attended college, my views of it can hardly be considered canonical, but I do know that it is the beginning of the rest of my life. In college, I look to learn my chosen trade (architecture), further my knowledge of the field, travel, meet new friends, and create a foundation for my life after college. For this to happen, I need to shed a lot of the skin that Fairport has placed on me. This is nothing new or particular to FHS, every high school has preconceptions; it comes with the age and maturity level that my peers and I are currently at. We judge, we shun, we see what we see through the eyes of others, rather than our own.

For example, I have met many, many kids at FHS. I have made it a point to talk and attempt to befriend everyone I have met. They come from all the different "groups", the "cool kids", the "nerds", the

75

"jocks", etc. One day, I was walking with a friend of mine, and I said hello to a kid that was in my English class. The friend I was walking with looked with a condescending look at me and said, "You talk to him? Isn't he on robotics?" To which I explained the other boy's amazing vocabulary, and funny sense of humor.

This experience made me realize something; a large majority of my classmates have not made the attempts to branch out that I have. My friend saw the other boy as just a "robotics kid", no one worthy of thinking about. I saw a hardworking student who had been with me for English for the last three years. It is this preconception that I cannot wait to cast away, because I know, though I may not do it, others do, and others do it to me as well.

I play tennis and ski race (hardly the most bad-ass sports). I get good grades, and I was accepted to school early decision (I get called an overachiever). My father is a successful, self-made businessman (a source of immense pride for me, but an excuse for others to view me as a "rich kid"). I know what people prejudge me on. I see it when my name is recognized upon introduction. It is for these reasons that I cannot wait to go to college and meet people who know nothing about me, of whom I know nothing about. This way, there will be nothing except their character and my character showing through. This is what high school lacks, and this is what I hope to achieve next year, and throughout my college career. In college, I will become the person I will be for the rest of my life, and I will meet the people who will help me realize those heights.

"The developmental assets are vital to our community's youth and an integral part of the community's recreation programming. Perinton is an engaged community where many groups work together for the good of the youth. Asset building is certainly one of these valued groups."

James Donahue,
Commissioner of Recreation and Parks, Town of Perinton

"It takes youth of real integrity to get involved in tasks that are difficult and of great magnitude, but that is just what the youth involved in asset building in Fairport-Perinton have done. As executive director of an organization that provides activities and services on-site at local low-income housing complexes, I have seen the positive impact asset building has had on the community and the youth involved."

Len Statham.
Executive Director of Partners in Community Development

Commitment to Learning

"I still care a great deal about my grades, as do many of the other girls on my team, and I try to do my best despite a very busy schedule."

Bailey Goodman

The Coloring Contest

By Alicia Loui

Once, in Jefferson Avenue School,

there was a coloring contest.

I was really excited.

I brang the sheet of

paper home so I could

color it. Then I started

coloring with my sisters.

My sisters colored

really good and I did

too.

But pretty soon I messed

up a little bit! I was

thinking that I wouldn t

win. I was sad.

Then nally I nished. After

that I ate dinner and brushed

my teeth, put on my pajamas,

and went to bed.

Then it waz the next morning and I

went to zchool. When I got

to zchool it waz time for

the morning announcement.

Then it waz time for the

people to announce the winnerz.

And one of the winnerz waz me!

I got to get a prize!

I waz happy and

proud of myzelf.

Why Do Teachers Give Us Homework?

By Reilly M. Mueller

Teachers give us homework because they want us to learn. I think it's important to learn because you don't want to be dumb. They want you to be smart. I know some of you don't like it, but homework is very, very important and healthy for your brain. When people get homework, everyone just goes, "Aw, man!!" and I just don't think that's acceptable. If your teacher gives you homework and you don't like it, you are just going to have to deal with it. I don't like homework either, but I do it anyway. If your teacher gives you homework and you purposely don't do it, you can get in a lot of trouble.

DO YOUR HOMEWORK!!!!!!!!!!!!!!!!!!!!!!!

I Love to Read

By Mary Sherman

I am sitting on my bed, reading late into the night. I flip the page vigorously, not waiting to see what happens next. I am at the climax of my book, anxiously waiting for the outcome.

I know that I should be asleep by now, but I just can't put my book down. Not yet. I love to read in my spare time. To me, reading is relaxing, something that I do when I want to block out everything else. I love reading books in which the words fit perfectly together, and they flow lightly across the pages. I feel a sense of accomplishment when I finish reading a book. I read for pure pleasure.

When I read, everything around me goes completely blank. I focus only on the book I am reading, tuning out everything else. I go into an imaginary world. I can imagine myself anywhere from the stars in the sky to deep in the ocean. When I read, I can go anywhere.

Reading can be so pleasurable. I read when I am bored, I read in my spare time, and I also read when I want to escape the real world. When I am stressed or sad, I read. But right now, I am reading just for fun.

My eyes start to hurt, they begin to burn. I don't know how much longer I can keep my eyes open. My eyelids are slowly closing, but I fight against it. I know I have to keep my eyes wide. I can't stop reading once I've started. I need to finish my book, no matter how long it takes. I will read into the morning if I have to.

When I pick up a book and start reading, I have to finish it. I won't allow myself to put down the book and stop reading it. There is no way. I get through books quickly, because I can never put them down. When I read the first sentence of a book, I get locked in. It's like there is an invisible force that is keeping my eyes on the pages.

I have only 30 pages left, I know that I can do it. I can't turn the pages fast enough. Only 20 pages left….. 10 pages….. 5…… 2…..

And finally, I feel that wonderful, pleasurable, sense of accomplishment that I strive for with every book I read. But now that I have finished, I want to pick up another book and start over again. I could read forever.

School

By Sumegha Juneja

Education, studying

Doing your homework,

Making friends,

Talking, listening,

Raising your hand,

Helping, caring

Lunch, English

Social Studies,

Science,

Math,

Spanish,

Teachers teaching,

Classrooms,

Positive attitude,

Wanting to be in school.

If There Were Twenty Five Hours in a Day

By Tara Schroth

If There Were Twenty Five Hours In A Day

by Tara Schroth

If there were twenty five hours in a day I would practice drawing for one hour sraight if I wasn't busy

If there were twenty five hours in a day my mom would make me do more math so I could improve in math.

I would like it if there were twenty five hours in a day because I would improve on everything.

The Lesson

By Zachary Navarro

Wednesday. The worst day of the week. Not because it meant that I still had another two days until the weekend, or because I had a math test, but because it was home to my weekly piano lesson.

As I pulled into the driveway, the sound of Bach could be heard permeating the walls of the small house, and would only get louder the closer I got to the purple door. As I slowly crossed the threshold into the house I dreaded so much, the mound of tightly curled grey hair could barely be seen over the grand piano. Mrs. Koots was waiting for me.

The bookshelf was filled with the heads of composers such as Beethoven, Chopin, and Mozart. The only sign of anything childhood related was the *Where's Waldo* book that sat tattered on the couch, waiting for someone to search for the man who had eluded so many.

Stepping further into the room and taking my seat next to Mrs. Koots, I would never have thought that this worn leather bench is where I would learn one of life's most important lessons.

Piano may not have come naturally to me, and it definitely was not what I wanted to spend 45 minutes working at every day, but the need to please Mrs. Koots forced me to work harder. If I messed up a scale, continuing was not an option. I would have to start from the beginning and repeat it until I got it right. If the peddling was wrong, no double pump would suffice.

Hard work is something that has traversed the walls of Mrs. Koots' house and entered into every part of my life. Whether it be hitting a grand slam during baseball, swishing a three pointer in a basketball game, or making it down the ski slope faster, hard work is how I accomplish my goals.

At school, the lessons learned while sitting alongside Mrs. Koots are present also. A poor grade is like a slap on the wrist with her ruler, reminding me that I must try harder and do better. A harsh criticism on a piece of work is similar to a disappointed glare over Mrs. Koots' wire framed glasses.

Without those disappointed looks or slaps on the wrists from Mrs. Koots, I would not have the skills or drive to work as hard as I do, and accomplish the goals for which I strive.

The 40 assets are essential to the success and development of our community and of students that live here. Creative activities better our lives in infinite ways, allowing us to express our thoughts and views in many outlets. These activities teach us the value of hard work, and allow us to see that success does not come without effort. As with Bailey, the 40 assets have been an integral part of my development, and I believe that each of these can be used to enhance the lives of the students and community members who apply them.

Books are Treasures

By Renee Weinstein

When you imagine a treasure box, you envision a petite golden chest, with pink crystals running haphazardly around the outskirts. It would be pulsing with happiness, the aura of joy shimmering around the box's perimeter. It would draw you near, pushing, pulling; begging you to open the container; and see for yourself what magic it's keeping captive. As soon as you delicately touch the box, the lid will creep open, revealing the objects hidden within. There, hidden beneath a sky blue blanket, is a mangled, damaged, and utterly hurt book. Your face would fall into an unmistakable frown, your beating heart slowing down to a moderate pace. With the disappointment pulsing and scrambling within, you snatch up the book, carefully opening up to the first page. Only then, only once you begin reading, will you realize what treasure really is.

To me, books are a fortune, an object you want to keep and protect. This treasure will always keep you company; a shadow following your every move. At the worst of times, your book, your companion, will be there; transporting you off into another realm. With books, it feels as if you leave all your problems behind, the inky black words running and running, agitating you to follow. Your friend can send you to a place where magic is true, and fairies dance to the rhythm of the wind. It can send you to a place where horses run wild, and beautiful flowers cover the meadows. Books encourage you to imagine, to dream, to push you to pursue what you want to achieve.

And the best thing about these helpers, these friends, these shadows, is that they will never leave you. You can *always* start them again.

Why We Have Homework

By Morgan Ingalls

By Morgan Ingalls

I think teachers give us homework beccause they want to grow our brains. Also, kids can have fun by learning. If there weren't teachers around, there would probably not be much learning. I know it's not always fun, but it's important. So this is why I think teachers give us home-work.

"A very important asset for me is "Bonding to School." This asset encompasses so many positive habits. Its success requires a connection from parents, teaches, coaches, counselors, directors, conductors, and the student. A student-school bond enriches all parties. In Fairport, a school-student bond is an asset that all students can successfully achieve."

Jon Hunter, Superintendent,
Fairport Central School District

"In Fairport we hold academics in the highest regard and strive for continued excellence in this realm. Grounded in research, we know the internal assets need to be a priority before academic success is realized. The acquisition of fundamental assets helps develop internal capacity so students can be contributors to our community and beyond. Place assets first and the rest will fall into place."

Brett Provenzano,
Principal, Johanna Perrin Middle School

Positive Values

"I also have a new perspective about money and don't take it for granted. It has made me question my values and what is truly important to me."

Bailey Goodman

A Lasting Effect

By Cole Bardreau

Sometimes we forget how far something so little can go. During my eighth grade school year in Auburn, New York, I was able to leave a lasting effect on a boy named Brandon.

Brandon was the same age as me and was a student in my mother's Special Education classroom. Brandon is mentally challenged but possesses a huge heart. He was extremely friendly and always tried to fit in and create friendships with students outside of my mom's classroom. Time after time he would be shut down and humiliated.

One day my mom proposed the idea of Brandon joining our lunch table for just a day. I agreed and didn't feel as if it would do any harm. Neither did my friends when the idea came up. The following day, I asked Brandon if he would like to sit with us in lunch. His face lit up like a pinball game and responded with a huge grin, "Yes, I would love to".

The next period Brandon stormed into the cafeteria and recovered his seat at the table. He was anything but shy and quick to immerse with my friends. He had the entire table laughing throughout lunch with his funny jokes and great sense of humor. I don't believe I will ever forget the smile he had on his face that day.

Following the bell to signal the end of the period, my friends swarmed me and practically begged me to invite Brandon back to the table. I respected their wishes and asked Brandon to sit with us again the next day. That was it; Brandon now occupied the little green chair next to me that was empty in previous weeks for the rest of the year.

As time went on more and more people were lucky enough to hear about Brandon. Everyone that actually gave Brandon a chance fell in love with him and his great personality. Whenever you saw Brandon in the halls he would either be making conversation or giving someone a high five. He was even able to build up enough confidence to come to school events such as my hockey games.

Now as I look back I realize that Brandon wasn't the only one that gained something. The entire school including myself was able to understand how important it is not to judge someone by how they look, but to take time and figure out who the person really is. I am tremendously grateful that I didn't pass the opportunity to have Brandon join our table.

Dear Elyse

By Cameron (Cami) Fletcher

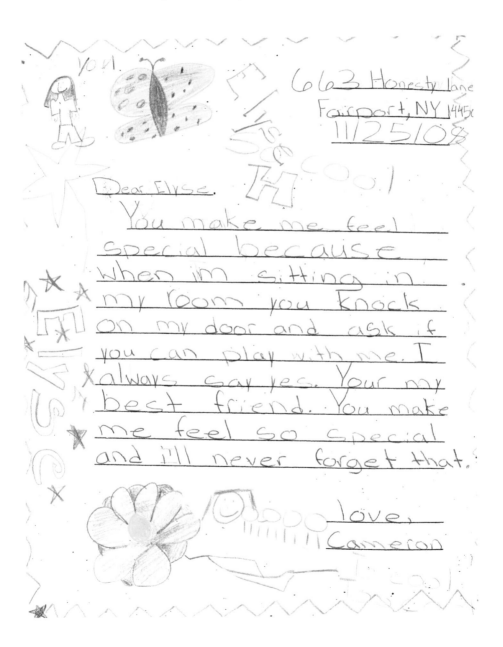

6663 Honesty lane
Fairport, NY 1445c
11/25/08

Dear Elyse,
You make me feel special because when im sitting in my room you knock on my door and ask if you can play with me. I always say yes. Your my best friend. You make me feel so special and i'll never forget that.

love,
Cameron

Conscience

By Andrew J. Goetz

Can you hear it inside you

Urging you to do

What you know to be true

Acting on behalf of others

You can hear the voice calling

As the evil smothers

The lives of men, children, and their mothers

Will you listen

Will you answer that call

To help others and therefore

Benefit us all

We have an obligation

In this nation

To fight for human salvation

Advice to a Fellow Teen...

By Valerie Senecker and Kaylie Hopkins

Reasons to restrain from being sexually active or using alcohol or drugs:

Enjoy being a teen without dealing with consequences from poor decisions

Safety- these actions can put the life as you know it at risk

Tragedy- participating in these activities can cause your family to deal with otherwise unnecessary heartbreak

Rules-the law and parents set rules to keep our youth safe and healthy

Anyone can give into peer pressure, but it takes true courage and self worth to stand by your decision to restrain

Integrity- the decisions you make in life, exhibit the morals you possess

Never change yourself or compromise your morals to be accepted. Stay true to yourself.

The Future- every decision you make in your teenage years will affect your future plans.

The affect could be negative or positive. Which course will you choose to take?

Memories

By David B. Collins

Past the vacant eyes and her blank stare

Lies a woman who was always there

With her once understanding silence

Now a mind in utter defiance

She slips farther away

The warm hugs

That welcoming smile

All the "I knows"

Seem to be only distant memories

Once shared, now only my own

She slips farther away

The sun drenched lunches on lazy afternoons

Long card games, in her living room

She slips farther away

My name, who I am

Forgotten from her mind

Lost somewhere

In the Depths of time

A flicker

A spark in her eye

And for a moment the memories return in a flood

Bringing with them her identity

She asks, "David! How are you?"

We are whole again

Life Lessons from Math Class

By Koby Green

It was a Thursday afternoon. It was ninth period math class with Mrs. Merritt. I sat at the desk closest to the door so I was first to notice the new kid walk in through the door. He was an average height African American that had moved here from Africa. The first thing I noticed when I saw him was how nicely he dressed. He wore nice dress pants with the crease all the way down the leg, also a nice button down shirt tucked in with a nice black belt. It must have been common to dress that way for school where he had come from, at least that's what I figured.

The new kid took a seat in the first open desk he saw. Mrs. Merritt started the lesson and then I didn't think much of him after that. We had a short lesson and then Mrs. Merritt broke us up into partners so we could work on a packet from the previous lesson. I worked with my buddy that I had met back in third grade and then with another kid I had just met this year.

As we started working I noticed the new kid was working alone. I asked my partners if they minded the new kid joining us, they seemed a little hesitant but I still went over anyway. I walked up to the new kid's desk and introduced myself. "Hey I'm Koby, what's your name man?" he answered with a humble, "Hey" and told me his name was Nuru. I asked if he would like to work with me and my friends, he immediately jumped to the opportunity and joined us. He sat down next to me and I introduced Nuru to my friends, who were now his new friends.

After we all met Nuru we got to work. We finished the first page pretty quick and were moving onto the next, I looked over at Nuru and noticed he was still on the first page. He looked at me and said "I don't really get this stuff" I asked Nuru if he wanted any help and he did not hesitate to accept. I started explaining the problem and took baby steps with him, then as we finished one problem, I would ease up on the help with the next problem, and I would keep doing this until he was at the point were he could do a whole problem on his own. The other two guys in my group kind of broke off and worked together while Nuru and I worked together, even though the other guys finished way before us. Nuru and I still finished the packet.

There was about seven or eight minutes left in the period, Nuru and I had finished the packet and we just started talking. I noticed a necklace he was wearing. It was a necklace shaped like Africa and it was almost in a knit form. I said it was a really cool necklace and he told me that he made it. He also told me a lot about Africa, his family and things he did in Africa. Like, play soccer work in his garden and hang out with his friends. Nuru also told me he was eighteen. I would have never guessed that he was eighteen, but I pretty much looked past it because friendship has nothing to do with age difference and I didn't think that his age changed how I looked at him or how he looked at me.

Nuru and I talked in school on a regular basis from that day forward. He eventually moved into a more advanced math class and I didn't see him much anymore. I will occasionally run into him in the hall ways and library but I feel the friendship is still there. I'll never forget the day I met Nuru, and saw that cool necklace.

Baxter

By Cierra Borcz

One day my Dad was reading the newspaper and saw there was a free dog to a good home. So, we rushed to the car and drove off. We were the first ones there. The day after, we got our dog. We named him Baxter. We were very happy.

A week after we named him he was hurt, so I told him to lay down and I looked at his paw. It had a thorn in it. So I pulled the thorn out and I kissed it. He felt much better.

After a year he tore up his cage and got out! Now he is fine and is himself again.

I LOVE MY DOG, BAXTER!!!!!

"I personally attended the national asset conference. On my return, I formed the Mayor's Youth Advisory Council as an opportunity for high school youth to serve on various village boards and committees. I am proud to know that I contributed to the spread of positive values through asset-building in Fairport and Perinton."

Clark King,
Mayor of Fairport, 1987-2006

Social Competencies

"Young people need to be connected to people of all ages for diverse viewpoints."

Bailey Goodman

A Good Friend

Written by the friends in
Mrs. Scheible's and Mrs. Smith's third grade class
Northside School
Fairport, N.Y.

A good friend cares for you.
A good friend asks you if you need help.
A good friend is a good sport.
A good friend plays with you on the playground.
A good friend makes you smile everyday.
A good friend doesn't have a bad attitude.
A good friend will support you in everything you do.
A good friend is always in your heart.
A good friend makes you feel better when you're sad.
A good friend can have a sleepover with you.
A good friend doesn't tell you what to do.
A good friend doesn't lie to you.
A good friend helps you make other friends.
A good friend never lets you down.
A good friend makes you happy.
A good friend shares with you.
A good friend is there for you.
A good friend stands up for you.
A good friend thinks you're special.
A good friend makes you laugh.
A good friend is someone you can trust and they can trust you. True

Life

By Riley Kaye

I always have to think ahead, because my parents are divorced. I can't always do what I want to do, like go somewhere with my friends. I also have to make the right choices every day in my life. I know I can lose or gain something by making choices. What I mean is, that if I make the wrong choice, I can get into a lot of trouble, but if I make the right choice everything can be OK. I learn from my mistakes. I have to think ahead about what clothes I should bring back and forth from my parents houses. I have to remember to keep an even amount of clothes at each house. My parents being divorced showed me how hard it is to lose someone you care about. This influenced me to help my friends if their parents are divorced or have lost a sibling.

My Role Model, Brent

By Livia C. Damiano

One of the strongest people I know is my brother Brent. Brent is mentally and physically disabled, he is 16 and goes to BOCES Creekside School. He is my role model.

In the past five years Brent has endured three major surgeries, the biggest one was the last. This surgery was performed in 2006 and involved back and spine surgery. The surgery itself took eight hours. After the operation Brent was in a tremendous amount of pain. He was so strong and he only cried once, the day after the surgery.

Brent has taught me how to be a stronger and better person. He's also taught me how to get through bad times. The bad things in the past that happened to me can't compare to what he has gone through. Even though he was in so much pain, he couldn't tell my parents if he needed help. But he didn't cry once! Also, Brent didn't even know what was going on or know why he was receiving the surgery.

I'm extremely proud of Brent. Even though he suffers from disabilities he still tries his best at everything he does. Last month my brother competed in Special Olympics for disabled kids. My brother bowled and took 6th place! Since Brent is unable to hold a bowling ball, the coordinators place a metal holder by his wheel chair. Then he rolls it down the ramp and into the alley.

I realize that he has been strong through lots of difficult times. Brent makes me a stronger person, and I love him.

How I Became

By Ulysses Miles

Many people view change in different ways, some fear and reject it while others hope for it. In my life, there has been one significant moment that caused me years of change. I have been to ten different schools and never really landed in a permanent settlement until 7th grade when I returned to Rochester to live with my uncle.

To lead up to my moment of change, my life started in Rochester, NY, in 1992. My original parents did not have the means to take care of me, so they put me up for adoption when I was a week old. This is how the Miles family adopted their second little boy. I was your average chubby little baby as hyper and hungry as ever. My father, William Miles was an avid baseball fan and my big brother, who was five at the time, took quickly to the sport. Though my father never smoked around my brother and me, smoking, if not baseball, was his most pleasurable hobby. Going on four years old at the time, I could never have experienced first hand the effects of smoking any clearer. Before the end of my first semester of daycare, smoking had given my father an impossible battle with lung cancer. This battle was lost before my fourth summer and would send my life in multiple directions.

Within two years, as I finished kindergarten, my mom moved my brother and me to Alabama to care for my elderly grandfather, who at the time was in his 80s. We switched back and forth from Catholic schools, to public school, to expensive schools. I never had much of a distinctive group of friends. This period of change comes across to many as depressing or sad, but for me it's opened my eyes at a young age. If not for these schools I would not have been involved with the numerous activities I have been in at Fairport High School. These include football, theater, track, various music, gymnastics, drumming, BMX biking, basketball, and the benefit of being able to connect to many different people with distinct personalities.

While this may not have had a negative effect on me, my mom, supporting us on her own was feeling the effects of stress. Two young energetic boys can take its toll on a single mother. At the end of my 6th grade year, my mother felt we would be better off with a male role model. She sent us off to live with our Uncle Jasper in Corn Hill, located near the center of Rochester. This brings about the end of my unstable childhood as I soon started attending Fairport High School.

During my period of change I learned how to communicate with different friends, from "skaters" to "jocks" and I still try to know at least one person from every group of friends. And while change has its pros and cons, it's a part of life everyone at some point will experience.

Tell the Teacher

By Ryan Gaudioso and Bryant Hinkley

Bryant Hinkley   Ryan Gaudioso

Tell the teacher them to brake it up

To, the kids were fighting on the playground over a play ball. No buts may pass with the

To kids were fighting on the playground over a playground ball. Then they found a game they both wanted to do. They decided to both play catch.

Rachel

By Lahra Sherwood

Way back on that cold blistery day I met Rachel. I was going to Mrs. L's classroom to help the kids during lunch. I started to go down in the beginning of the year. Every day I went down, and everyday she was sitting there waiting for me. I became good friends with her. Even though she had a learning disorder, I loved going down to see her. She had the biggest, friendliest smile.

One day I saw a boy calling her rude, inappropriate names. I ran over and had him stop. He finally left, and I hugged Rachel. I asked her if she wanted to come over to my house. Rachel said that she would ask her mom. Later that day Rachel's mom dropped her off at my house. Rachel wanted to watch the movie Aladdin. I popped popcorn, and Rachel started the movie. She was very grateful for my kindness. I told her that I was glad that she was my friend. I had her over whenever I could. She was overjoyed when she came over.

I went to her house one afternoon and Rachel told me that she was moving to Pennsylvania. I asked her if I could have her new address and phone number. Later that week Rachel told me that she was moving in two weeks. I decided that I would spend as much time as I could. My mom thought that I should get her a goodbye present. I went to the store and bought her a friendship bracelet.

On her last day I gave the bracelet. Rachel gave me a big hug and told me that she would never forget me. I wanted to cry, but I knew that I would be able to keep in contact. She moved, and I wrote everyday. I am glad that I was able to meet her. She was my best friend. I thought about her every day.

Rachel wrote me a letter saying that she was moving back to New York. I wrote back telling her that I would be waiting for her. I called her asking when she would arrive. She told me that she would be arriving in one hour. My mom drove me to the airport and there I met her in a big bear hug. Rachel told me all about Pennsylvania, and how her dad couldn't find a job. I was really excited to have her back. She was excited to be back. Although she has found other friends, I still talk to her today.

Confessions of a Skeleton

By Alyssa Carolyn Monheim

For years, I wanted to be barely visible,

less defined.

a skeleton.

I used to slave over this idea of perfection.

Our world is built purely on the exterior.

See how we compare to the person next to us.

Skinnier, prettier?

Well, let's get something straight,

You win.

I can't begin to explain the war inside my head.

I still fight it.

I wanted control,

Losing everything else, I needed that sense of power.

Power to push away the plate. Power to refuse.

Somewhere along the road

I realized I didn't have it,

I lost control.

I stripped myself

and begin to remold,

to pick up my pieces.

to start over.

I don't measure up to people's standards,

In fact I don't feel I meet my own.

But I'm learning,

trying,

believing

I've grown because of myself.

Lessons in Diversity

By Angela Wang

Looking out the bus window, I watched flashes of green whiz by. It was still strange to see so many trees in one place. Back in China, the horizon had been covered by towering skyscrapers and a thick coat of smog. Since I'd arrived in Boston a month ago, everything was new and unusual. But today was especially remarkable; I was six years old, and it was my first day of first grade. Now as I stepped off the bus, my breath caught. I gazed up at the single-story brick school with crowds of kids milling around outside. It looked welcoming enough, but it still took me a few minutes to muster up the courage to go in.

My classroom was just around the corner, and a smiling lady came out just as I peered in. She was tall and slender, with chin length blond hair and laugh lines at the corners of her twinkling eyes.

"Hello," she said, smiling down at me. "I'm Ms. M. You must be Angela. How do you like the U.S. so far?"

"Um…fine," I mumbled, looking down at my shoes.

Ms. M. led me into the brightly lit room. There were rows of cubbies along the back wall and large bins of crayons and markers. The desks were arranged in groups of four, and she led me to an open desk next to a little blond girl.

As soon as I sat down, the girl turned to me, a cheery grin lighting up her face.

"Hi, I'm Suzanne. You're Angela and you're new. Ms. M. said you just got here from China. That is so cool. What was it like there? Do you eat with chopsticks? Have you ever seen a panda? Do you have any siblings? I have a brother and sister. Do you move around a lot? I've lived here my whole life…"

Her interest and sunny mood was infectious. I soon found myself asking about her life. She told me that she played soccer and visited her grandparents on weekends. This was strange to me, since my grandparents lived in another city and I hardly ever saw them. I also thought it strange that she owned a dog, since scarcely any people owned dogs in China.

During recess that day, I was the most popular target for questioning. The other kids were curious about my culture, and in turn, I discovered a lot about American culture.

A few months later, I went to Suzanne's birthday party. Her parents had gotten Chinese food, the kind in cartons with chopsticks. Everyone seemed astounded that I could use them and were delighted to learn. Later that night, I experienced my first movie and popcorn night.

I'm so glad that I had the experience I did in Boston. I learned so much about American culture, which became very helpful when I moved to Fairport later that year. I also helped my fellow classmates experience Chinese culture, from its foods to its customs. Looking back today, I realize that those few months have taught me to appreciate many other cultures and made me a better, more considerate person.

"I believe the single most important program we have done for Minerva DeLand students in my 12 years as principal is Leadership Asset Training. This work has made a noticeable difference in the climate of our building. Our students are better community citizens, friendlier to each other and appear to value the support from their peers to make healthy choices."

Patrick Moriarty,
Principal, Minerva DeLand School

Positive Identity

"I have a more realistic view of life and understand that life is full of disappointments but also triumphs."

Bailey Goodman

What I Live For

By Bryanna Ellis

When I wake up everyday,
I don't decide to be where I am.
But I do decide
What I live for,
What I can look forward to.
I live
To see the happiness of my family.
I live
For the value of friendship, my best friends.
I live
To hear music,
I live
To see myself succeed.
I live
To travel the world,
To have an exciting journey,
To never get too comfortable because nothing is ever constant.
I live
To help others,
To break the walls of ignorance.
I live
For the belief in humanity.
I live
To be the best person I can be,
To make the best memories,
And to love with all my heart.
I live

To witness the miracles of everyday

Who You Are

By Mitchell Anderson

The important thing to remember in order to survive high school is not to do your homework, or how to write an introduction to a thematic essay, nor is it to suck up to your teachers. The most important thing to remember is to not forget who you are.

Obviously I am not talking about your name. I am talking about where you came from and what you value in this world. And if you don't know what you value then you had better figure it out because things are about to get confusing. The reason you need to figure this out right now is because there are going to be people, not only in high school, but throughout your life that are going to tell you that you are not okay. They are going to tell you this, and ridicule you because you are different. They will question your beliefs and torment you to no end. I don't care who you are, it's going to happen to you.

The worst part about all this is that these people are not going to be strangers; they are going to be your friends, your teachers, and maybe even your parents. I'm here to tell you not to listen to them! I'm here to tell you that you are fine just the way you are. I am fifteen years old and I have experienced some horrible things, things I hope none of you ever have to deal with, and throughout your life I want you to remember one thing, even if it means knowing nothing else. This world is a beautiful place, filled with beautiful things! Don't be fooled, this world can be a very cold and dark place and at times you are going to feel like giving up! You are going to think that your life is horrible and that things will never get better, but believe me when I tell you that they will. No matter how dark it gets it will always get better. And if you have the strength to see through that darkness than you will experience great and wonderful things and nothing will be able to stand in your way.

Purpose

By Alicia Yamashita

Making a Difference

By Miranda Sambuchi

I feel that everyone has a purpose in life. Some people are teachers because they want to help children. Some people are therapists because they want to help people of all age feel better about themselves. Some little kids without even knowing make other people feel good by simply smiling at them. No one should ever feel like they are a waste of space, even if you don't know it yet, there's a purpose for your life.

I know what I'm going to be when I grow up. I'm going to be a teacher, but that's not it. I'm going to be the teacher that everyone feels comfortable with, and everyone knows that they can talk to. If I can help one person by the time I'm gone my life has been worth living. I feel like I'm the kind of person that would talk to someone if they were lonely, help them pick up their books if they dropped them, or even give them my number to help them study if they asked. My mother is known as the teacher that kids know they can talk to. She is my role model. She works at Jefferson Avenue and when she wakes up in the morning she thinks of one way she could possibly help someone.

If everyone looked out for everyone, then we'd live in a perfect world. That's obviously not the case, so even if you think you're one person and you can't make a difference, you're wrong. By you being a good person, you're one less person putting people down in this world, and have made a difference.

I Felt Proud

By Micaela Brigida

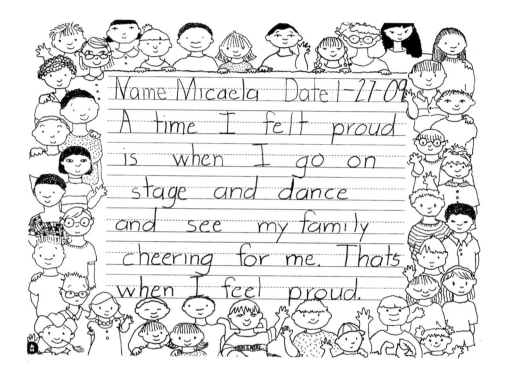

Name Micaela   Date 1-27-09
A time I felt proud
is when I go on
stage and dance
and see my family
cheering for me. Thats
when I feel proud.

When I Am Biking

By Anonymous

It's winter now. Many people consider it long past the time to pull out the bikes for a joyful excursion, but I disagree. As soon as my foot hits the pedal, everything else falls away. My body, already tired from basketball practice, nevertheless looks forward to the chilly ride home. It's dark out and my way is lit by the occasional streetlamp and the headlights of passing cars. But I know the way. I know where to avoid catching a tire on a curb. I know where tree roots push up the sidewalk and form dangerous bumps. I know where puddles are likely to form, or patches of ice, and I know where poles pose a threat if I don't slow down enough for a turn.

As my hands grip the bars, my fingers start to go numb, regardless of whether or not I'm wearing gloves. The wind blasts against my face and chills my leg, but the cold only makes me feel more alive. I breathe it in, refreshing crispness unlike any other time of year. As I push up a hill, the icy wind dulls the burning complaints of my muscles. My lungs feel as if they are about to be ripped open by an icy dagger, but when I reach the top a wave of accomplishment washes over me, eclipsing the feeling of fatigue. I push ever onward, my legs stopping their cyclic motion only when I come to intersections and traffic lights.

The rhythmic movement of my legs produces a low hum from the bike, constant and easy. In the cold night this sound is reassuring, soothing. All is quiet, but for this cadenced hum. No one is yelling, even my thoughts grow quiet. My mind is filled by this sound, by the motion of my legs, and by the winter night around me. If thoughts of other things come to me, they are easy and fluid. I consider the homework I have to do when I get home, or my schedule for the next day, and then the thoughts slip neatly into the place in the back of my mind.

I feel I have somehow cheated the world. I have turned the oppression of night, snow, and cold into a tranquil experience of reflection. It has been during these wintry excursions that I have had some of my most meaningful realizations. I put things in perspective, knowing that sometimes to get ahead I must slow down. I look at a situation from different points of view and come to terms with it. I realize things about myself, or my family, that I had not realized before. I consider why I am here, and look inside myself to realize I am content with not knowing why, but determined to never stop wondering. Wondering about the big picture keeps me from worrying about the small.

If I go for an extended period of time without biking, things build up and threaten to overwhelm. Biking makes everything right again. It is my release, simple but essential. When I am angry, biking soothes me. When I am weary from the world, it makes me feel awake and alert. When I am depressed, the air breathes new life into me. When I want to cry, only my bike is there to witness the falling tears, and cannot judge. When I am happy, I pedal faster and the speed invigorates me even more. Going down hills, the wind rushing past me makes me feel as if I am flying. I stand up to pedal and tower over the world, ready to conquer the road ahead. When I am biking, nothing else matters, just the strain of my muscles, the hum of the tires, and the energy of the air.

In the Future

By Valerie Francis

In the future, where will you be?
Exploring the world? Or home with children of three?
It's a lifelong process, to figure it out,
Just think positive, and have no doubt.
People will try to stop you from being who you are,
Ignore those people, and you will go far.
Curly hair wants straight hair, blond wants to be brunette,
Accept who you are, if they don't like you, it's their threat.
Have confidence in your abilities and don't put yourself down,
Your capable of anything, make a difference in this town.
Please remember, it's all up to you,
Your future, itself, and the life you live too.

Positive Leadership

By Isaiah Cuffee Martine Patterson Smith

I am Isaiah Smith of Jefferson Avenue School. I am in 4th Grade. This month we are all working on positive leadership. The thing that I am writing about is being positive and helpful. Someone around the world might be in trouble. If there is something you are good at you can do anything you put your mind to. Take me for example. My idol is Terrell Owens, Wide Receiver for the Dallas Cowboys. Take one good look at me and I don't think I am going to get there and one day I said ''Isaiah look at your self. If you try hard you will get there.'' So the moral of this is do anything you put your mind to!!!!

Voice

By Alli Myers

"You Jew." I think about this phrase for a moment as I sit chewing on my peanut butter and jelly sandwich. I am a Jew. But why does he always say it in such a derogatory tone? The past week has been the same. Everyday I come to school. Everyday I watch the clock's hands slide together over twelve noon. Everyday I clutch my brown paper bag and follow the mass of students to the stuffy, loud cafeteria. Everyday I sit down and open my bag. I'm usually halfway through my sandwich when I can hear him. And today is no different. What I don't understand is what triggered it. Earlier last week in class we were discussing holidays. When we got to Hanukkah my teacher asked if anyone in the class celebrated it. I raised my hand and realized I was the only one in the room. At first I felt pride, until he cracked a joke. But why did he continue? Had he seen my cheeks burn red that day? My thinking is interrupted when I hear a penny drop to the ground.

"Aren't you going to snatch at it? Or can you out stand your greed." I'm trying out a new strategy. Maybe if I don't look at him. Maybe if I give him the money in my bag it will show him I am generous…

"Well are you? Here I'll throw another." A second coin clinks to the ground. I watch it spin on the floor, to see which way it lands. Tails. I glance at the classmates sitting with me. Their mom's must have become the ultimate lunch makers within the past week because boy, did they all seem silent and oh-so-fascinated with their bologna sandwiches. Why couldn't he just harass someone Christian? Someone… Buddhist? Am I all that different? Does he hate me this much? I retrace all the events that had happened prior to this. I never said anything wrong. I never said anything mean to him. Is it really only because I'm Jewish? Why am I sitting here allowing him to make me feel ashamed? I stand up.

"Oh no guys it looks like she's making a move for all the

money I have. Aren't you rich enough?" I was just going to throw out my trash. I wasn't even going to say anything. But in that moment I think of my family. I think of my heritage. I think of who I am. And somehow, I found my voice.

What I Live For

By Rachael Palmer

Every morning when I awake,

I choose something

To look forward to.

It can be as trivial as eating ice cream for breakfast,

Or something like traveling to a new place.

This world has so many new and exciting things to offer.

Take advantage of them.

Live for the things in life that

Challenge

Change

And Affect

The way you see the world

And how you live your life.

I Won My Swim Meet

By Anna E. LaPoint

Anna E. LaPoint

I was proud when I won my swim meet!

Purpose

By Katie Johnson

I feel like I am here for a purpose. If I could choose one from a list, I would choose helping others. One thing that I love doing is helping others, and making a difference in people's lives. Ever since an early age I have been called to help others, mainly through church. The feeling that I get when I help someone and make a difference in their life is the best feeling in the world!

When I was in middle school I started participating in an event called the 30 hour famine. We raised money for kids in different countries that don't receive any food at all. This really opened my eyes to see that I could put forth so much more! I knew that I wanted to be involved in many more activities that helps others! Since then I have participated in many things. A big example of helping others that I do and love is doing service through Reach Workcamps. My youth group travels to different places every summer and we fix up homes of people who are either physically or financially unable to do so themselves. These residents that we help are the nicest people you will ever meet and they appreciate it much more than we will ever know. With a house suitable for living, they can now go out and help others make a difference.

Big projects like this aren't the only way to help others, even the small things count. By helping someone pick up their note cards in the hallway can give them a smile that will last the rest of the day. Or by saying "Hey, what's up?" to a new student can really make them feel welcomed and accepted!

Helping others is my passion. I am hoping to go out into the world and continue this throughout my life!

What Is Hope?

By LaRoyce Lawson

Hope is the thing that lets us thrive

Hope is something that keeps us alive

Hope is the force that makes you achieve

Hope is the spirit that makes you believe

Hope makes you live through the day

Hope makes you live in a new way

Hope can make the whole world change

Hope can make a person's life rearrange

Hope can bring you through any drama

Hope can solve a person's trauma

Hope can come from anywhere

Hope is everywhere

Hope can come from many places

Hope is in all places

Hope is all you need to do

It's up to me and it's up to you

I Felt Proud

By Erik J. Morrow

Name Erik   Date 1-17-09
I felt proud because
I was rideding my
new bike. And I fell
of. And ansted of siting
there I walked back
home.

About Me

By Hannah Louise Congdon

I like to smile, be loud and bubbly

But there is more to me than what you see

I am not just a cheerleader who's really preppy.

I believe I am here to make a difference

To help those who need it the most.

To give them strength and comfort when it is needed.

I miss the times when I could sleep forever

And had no worries in the world.

I could play all day and just be me.

I fear the world I do not know

And what only time will tell.

I don't like not knowing what happens next

Or what is in store for my future.

I love to love.

I think all the world needs is love

And for everyone to get along.

I don't like war and hope for peace on Earth.

I hate when people don't get along

Or fight over stupid reasons.

Life is too short to be caught up in drama.

I wish people would treat others with respect.

Listen when they are talking

And don't talk while they are talking.

I like to be known as a cheerleader

But there is more to me than that.

I hope to someday make a difference in the world

So it will be a better place for everyone.

Peace, Love, Happiness.

"This book of reflective pieces and illustrations by student and community members is a wonderful way to encourage youth in our community to be positive role models."

Rep. Louise Slaughter, NY-28

Bailey's Book Committee

Bailey Goodman's family and several of her friends met regularly to conceive, develop, and execute the plan for *Bailey's Book: A Community Celebrates Its Assets*. They are:

Sandra Beckwith

Dillan Clement

Joshua Dillon

Ali Fitzgerald

Michael Goodman

Sharon Goodman

Spencer Goodman

Molly Kehoe

Heather Knowles

Krystal Newcombe

Samantha Nunn

Jackie Pinto

Joelle Pinto

Irene Poray

Bill Poray

Debra Tandoi